THE WAORANI
PEOPLE OF THE ECUADORAN RAIN FOREST

THE WAORANI

PEOPLE OF THE ECUADORAN RAIN FOREST

by

A L E X A N D R A   S I Y

DILLON PRESS
New York

Maxwell Macmillan Canada
Toronto

Maxwell Macmillan International
New York Oxford Singapore Sydney

ACKNOWLEDGMENTS

My sincere thanks to Dr. James A. Yost, who lived with the Waorani for ten years and whose research has contributed a great deal to our knowledge of this once-isolated people. I am most grateful for the guidance and information he provided to me.

I also wish to thank Linda Belamarich of Cultural Survival, Kate E. Broyles and Linda T. Covington of Maxus Energy Corporation, Michael Gallagher of the Summer Institute of Linguistics, Fabian Garces of Petroecuador, Polly Mathewson of Survival International, and Vawter Parker of the Sierra Club Legal Defense Fund, Inc.

My gratitude also goes to the reference librarians at the Bethlehem Public Library in Delmar, New York, for their help in obtaining materials.

And for their patience and love during the writing of this book, I thank my husband, Eric, and my young daughter and son.

PHOTO CREDITS

All photos courtesy of Dr. James A. Yost except for the image on page 47, courtesy of Stephen Corry/ Survival International.

"The Spider Monkey's Tail," "The Origin of Cassava," "The Rainbow," and "The Origin of the Corn Bees" have been published here with the gracious permission of the publisher, the Summer Institute of Linguistics, Inc., from *Workpapers Concerning Waorani Discourse Features*, edited by Evelyn G. Pike and Rachel Saint, copyright 1988

Book design by Carol Matsuyama.

LIBRARY OF CONGRESS CATALOGING-IN-PUBLICATION DATA

Siy, Alexandra.
    The Waorani : people of the Ecuadoran rain forest / by Alexandra Siy. – 1st ed.
       p. cm. – (Global villages)
    Includes bibliographical references.
    Summary: Describes the culture and plight of the Waorani, an indigenous tribe of the Ecuadoran rain forest whose environment and way of life are threatened by the encroachment of the industrial world.
    ISBN 0-87518-550-9
    1. Huao Indians–Juvenile literature. [1. Huao Indians. 2. Indians of South America–Ecuador.]
I. Title II. Series.
F3722.1.H83S59   1993
986.6'00498–dc20
                                                      92-36985

Dillon Press
Macmillan Publishing Company
866 Third Avenue
New York, NY 10022

Maxwell Macmillan Canada, Inc.
1200 Eglinton Avenue East
Suite 200
Don Mills, Ontario M3C 3N1

Macmillan Publishing Company is part of the Maxwell Communication Group of Companies.

First edition

Printed in the United States of America

10   9   8   7   6   5   4   3   2   1

CONTENTS

INTRODUCTION

As the 1990s draw to a close, we look forward to not only a new century but a new millennium. What will the next thousand years bring for the planet earth and its people? And what aspects of our ancient past will we retain on our journey into a new time, a new world?

Today the world is already a vastly different place from what our great-grandparents would have imagined. People from distant parts of the planet can communicate within seconds. In less than 24 hours, you can fly around the world. Thanks to these and other remarkable advances in technology, the world has become a "global village."

In a sense, the peoples of the earth are no longer strangers, but neighbors. As we meet our "neighbors," we learn that now, more than ever before, our lives are intertwined. Indeed, our survival may depend on one another.

Deep in the rain forests of Ecuador, a people known as the Waorani have, until recently, lived their days in the same ways that their ancestors did for thousands of years. Isolated in the jungle, the Waorani made their first peaceful contact with the outside world only 35 years ago. If the modern industrial world did not have such a pressing need for new sources of energy–and if population growth were not skyrocketing worldwide–the Waorani would have remained undisturbed in their ancestral lands. And this book would not have needed to be written.

But oil exploration is threatening the survival of this ancient people. Roads are being built in the jungle, opening the land to settlers. And the forest itself–rich in marvelous forms of life–is also in jeopardy.

Being part of a global village need not be a bad thing. While the Waorani may not be totally pleased to have been "discovered," they have benefited in some ways from contact with modern societies. And those of us who live in industrialized nations may find that being part of a global village broadens our view of not only the world but our own culture. As we get to know our neighbors, we may even find new ways to understand and respect all people.

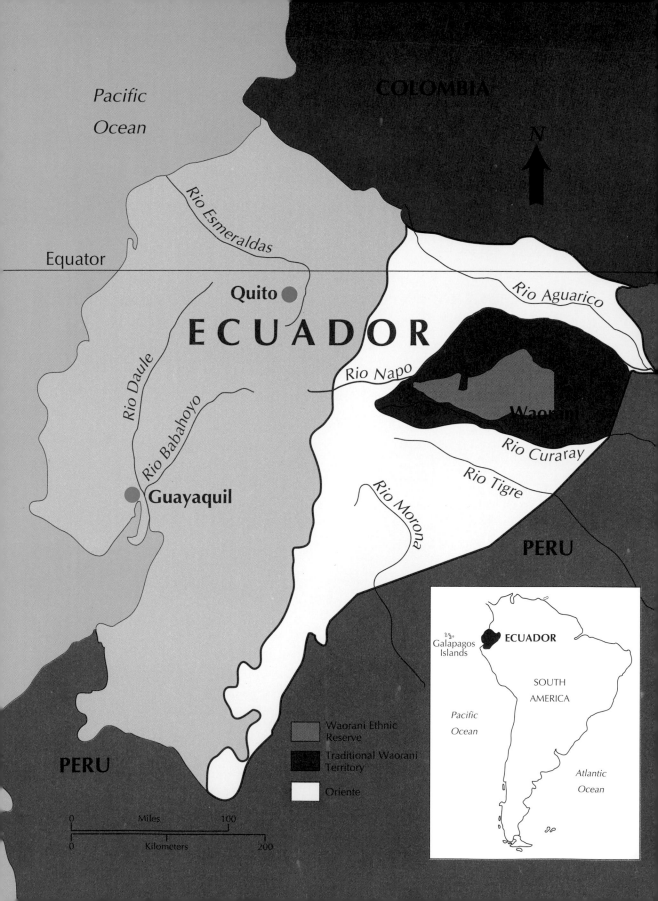

FAST FACTS

CULTURE
Farming, hunting, and gathering foods in the tropical rain forests of eastern Ecuador.

HUMAN HISTORY
Anthropologists think the Waorani have lived isolated in the jungle for many centuries. First contacts with the outside world probably occurred in the 1600s, when Waorani were kidnapped, murdered, or enslaved by the Spanish. The first peaceful contact was made in 1958.

NATURAL HISTORY
The Ecuadoran rain forests are ancient. Scientists estimate South American soils are more than 180 million years old.

GEOGRAPHY
The Waorani live in the rain forests of eastern Ecuador in a region known as the Oriente, part of Amazonia. Waorani territory traditionally covers about 8,100 square miles of forests between the Napo River and the Curaray River.

CLIMATE
Humid and warm all year, averaging between 70°F and 85°F; the area receives about 120 inches of rainfall a year.

GLOBAL IMPORTANCE
The Waorani are an ancient tribe who until recently used only Stone Age tools. Their unique culture, along with the tropical rain forests, is threatened by oil exploration, logging, tourism, mining, and colonization.

CURRENT STATUS
American and other foreign oil companies continue to drill for oil in Ecuador and are proposing new drilling sites on Waorani lands.

A young Waorani hunter with his catch. Monkeys live high in the rain-forest canopy, usually more than 100 feet above the ground.

CHAPTER ONE

THE WAORANI—THE PEOPLE

Weene doodani apaenegadanipa—"Long, long ago the ancestors told this story. . . ."

THE SPIDER MONKEY'S TAIL

Long, long ago the spider monkey was sitting high in a tree with his long tail. When the Waorani came to swim in the river, the spider monkey would rush out, grab them by wrapping his long tail around their throats, and drag them under the deep water. He held them under a long time, and when they died he uncurled his tail. When he let go, the dead bodies surfaced. They floated on the water.

Later on some other Waorani decided to go swimming. When they laughed and yelled, as they always did when they went swimming, the spider monkey rushed in and grabbed a Waorani by wrapping his tail around his throat and pulled him down under the water. The monkey held him under for a long time. When he was dead, the monkey released his tail and the corpse surfaced.

When the Waorani realized that they were dying off a few at a time by being drowned, one man said, "Now I am going to the place at the river where the spider monkey drowns us and I am going to cut off his tail!" When he decided that, another Waorani, taking the chonta-palm club, which he sharpened, fastened a vine very tightly across the river.

The two Waorani then went swimming at the place where the vine was stretched. The spider monkey ran out and fastened his tail around one man's neck and tried to pull him under. But the man grabbed hold of the vine and held his head above the water. The monkey was unable to pull the man under, and the other man grabbed the spider monkey from behind. Then the first Waorani reached out and cut off his tail. And it fell into the water.

After that happened, another monkey came with the same intention. The crazy monkey! He grabbed a Waorani, but since the vine was fastened in the same way, one of the men grabbed him. Then, as they did before, someone cut off his tail. The spider monkey went high up into the treetops.

Never again did the spider monkeys secretly grab and drown people at the river. And the spider monkeys long ago became dwellers of the treetops and no longer lived beside the rivers.

STORIES

The Waorani (pronounced wow-RON-ee) are a people who live in the rain forests of eastern Ecuador. They have lived in these remote forests for many centuries–no one knows how long. The people tell many stories about their history, but they do not know where they originally came from. They simply say that they came from down the river a long time ago.

The Waorani had no written language until about 1970. Learning and knowledge were found in a total way of living, or **culture**. Their culture is still described in stories the people have told for generations.

Stories contain important information. They are also good sources of entertainment. People enjoy listening to and learning stories so that they can be told again and again down through the years.

In some parts of the world, such as North America, **fossils** and ancient tools tell stories about the people who lived in an area. But in the tropical rain forests, fossils and other clues about the past are very rare because wooden tools and bones decay quickly in the warm and humid environment, leaving no trace behind.

The Waorani language is the only clue scientists have that might explain the origin of the people and how long they have been around. Their language is so different from any other in the world that most scientists believe the Waorani have been isolated from other people for hundreds and maybe thousands of years. Their word for themselves, Waorani, means simply "the people."

NATIVE LANDS

The Waorani live in a place known as the Oriente. This area of Ecuador is part of the vast region of Amazonia, which covers 2 million square miles of tropical rain forests surrounding the Amazon River and its tributaries. Waorani territory covers about 8,100 square miles of rain forests bordered by the Napo and Curaray rivers.

The Waorani are a seminomadic people. This means they move their villages every few months to a different part of the forest but return to the same places every year. Their movement is influenced by the availability of animals for hunting and palm leaves for building houses. It is also influenced by their practice of shifting cultivation, or gardening in several places. Traditionally, the Waorani have lived together in small groups ranging from about 10 to 30 people. Today there are still many small groups scattered in the forest, but some people are settling in permanent villages.

In the past the Waorani avoided living near riverbanks, where footprints could be left behind. It was feared that footprints would lead outsiders or hostile Waorani groups to a village. The Waorani often attacked one another in spearing raids. To reduce the chances of attack, the Waorani built their huts and planted their gardens in the hills away from the rivers.

Today the Waorani no longer kill one another in spearing raids. Several permanent villages have been established near the

Traditionally, the Waorani have lived in small, isolated communities scattered throughout the rain forest.

rivers, where the land is more fertile. Now, instead of walking to their gardens, they travel to them by canoe. The gardens also can be planted more frequently because the land along the rivers is much richer than the hillside soil.

"FIRST" PEOPLE

The Waorani are **indigenous** people–also known as original, aboriginal, native, tribal, or first people. Indigenous people are the descendants of the first people to live in an area. Their ancient connection to the land has helped them form beliefs about the earth. For example, like most indigenous tribes in Amazonia, the

15

THE WAORANI

Waorani believe that land cannot be owned. Instead, they believe that people belong to the land and have a responsibility to care for it, for the land provides them with everything they need to survive.

Among the Waorani there are no leaders. The people share everything–food, housing, and responsibilities for raising children. Their society is **egalitarian**, one in which all people are equal.

VIOLENT TIMES

The Waorani lived isolated in the forests for centuries until the 1600s, when Europeans came to the area. Stories tell of Waorani being shot and killed. Some were kidnapped and sold as slaves. By the late 1800s, **rubber gatherers** were invading Waorani territory. They also murdered the native people or sold them into slavery. The Waorani continued to clash with outsiders, or *cowodi*, well into the 20th century.

In the 1940s oil exploration began in the Oriente, and violent encounters erupted between oil workers and Waorani. In 1956 **missionaries** flew into Waorani territory, hoping to make peaceful contact with the people. But the five young missionaries who were sent were speared to death by the Waorani.

Until recently the Waorani believed that all *cowodi* were cannibals with bulging eyes and hands like frogs' feet. *Cowodi* were thought to be the sons of the giant anaconda snake.

The Waorani did not restrict their attacks to *cowodi*, however. They often attacked other Waorani groups, sometimes spearing everyone in a village. The reasons for the attacks are difficult for non-Waorani to understand. Often people were speared for revenge. The Waorani believed that if something bad happened, such as the death of a child, it was caused by another Waorani who they thought held a grudge against the family. That person was supposed to possess supernatural powers that he used against the child. His family group, then, was attacked for revenge.

The way the Waorani lived, in small isolated groups throughout the jungle, also contributed to the hostility. Often a group would become worried about being attacked by a neighboring group of Waorani. One of the groups would raid the other to avoid being attacked first.

Fear, anxiety, and grief were always part of Waorani life. For generations, however, the people actually wanted to end the killings. But peace was difficult to achieve because the Waorani moved around so much and because they had no leaders to bring them together.

THE MISSIONARIES

Finally, in 1958, two missionary women made the first peaceful contact with some of the Waorani. They were accompanied by a Waorani woman named Dayome. Dayome had fled her village 11 years earlier during a spearing raid made on her family by

Making a spear. For centuries, the Waorani killed one another in spearing raids. Today they are a peaceful people, and the spears they make are used to kill wild pigs or catch fish.

another group of Waorani. For years she lived with the Quichua, a different native tribe, in a distant village in Amazonia. Dayome's return with the *cowodi* reassured the people enough to trust the missionary women.

Until the missionaries came, the Waorani believed that the entire world was a rain forest surrounded by a circle of water. Tilted up on the west, rivers flowed through the forests toward the rising sun. Contact with the outside world has changed this belief, along with many others.

During the 1960s missionaries began living with the Waorani. Their goal, or mission, was to teach the people about Christ. Some

Waorani accepted Christianity although they held on to many of their traditional spiritual beliefs as well. They had, indeed, always believed in an afterlife and a creator, or god, called Waengongi.

The Waorani say the most important message brought to them by the missionaries was the message of peace. Christian teachings helped them to stop their vengeful acts and bring peace to their community. Today only about 20 percent of the Waorani are Christians. But nearly all Waorani have been influenced by the missionaries. Along with their religious teachings, the missionaries brought modern tools and clothing. Many Waorani accepted these new items, regarding them as labor-saving and helpful.

THE OIL RUSH

Oil exploration continued in the Oriente in the 1960s. Little by little the Waorani were pushed into smaller and smaller areas of the forests. In 1968 missionaries began to move many of the Waorani by airplane to a special area 620 square miles in size. Known as the "protectorate," this land is a place similar to an Indian reservation in the United States.

Only Waorani are allowed to enter and live on the protected lands. But the Ecuadoran government has the right to all the minerals and resources lying below the rain-forest floor. Therefore, the government can drill for oil on land that is "legally" Waorani territory.

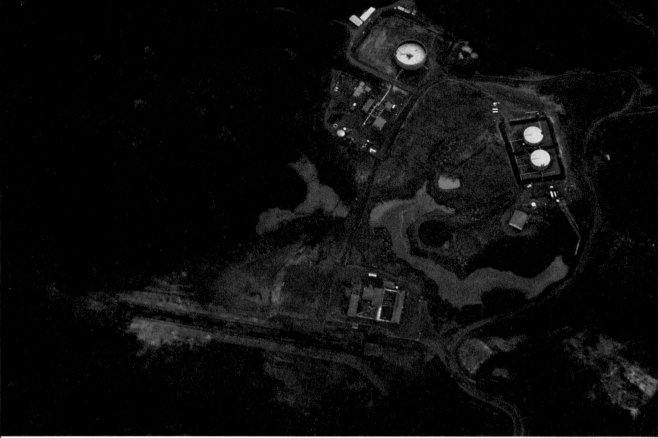

Oil fields like this one are threatening to destroy the land and way of life of the Waorani.

Some groups concerned with the welfare of the Waorani have accused the missionaries of helping the Ecuadoran government and the oil companies. They claim that the missionaries moved the Waorani to the protectorate so that the oil companies could explore the forests without interference by the Waorani. The missionaries, they say, have contributed to the destruction of Waorani lands.

The protectorate was only a small fraction of traditional Waorani land and could not provide food and homes for all the people. Recognizing this, some of the missionaries tried to help the Waorani regain their ancestral lands. However, government officials and some people from other tribes didn't want the Waorani to have so much land. After 16 years of efforts by many groups and individuals, the Waorani succeeded in recovering some of their land. In 1990 the protectorate was enlarged to include 2,000 square miles of original Waorani territory. This "Waorani Ethnic Reserve" comprises about one-quarter of traditional Waorani land, and nearly all of the people live on it.

In the early 1960s there were about 500 Waorani scattered in groups throughout the rain forests. Today the population has tripled—mainly because the Waorani no longer kill one another in spearing raids. But the survival of the Waorani is threatened. And in the long run, the new weapons of destruction are much more powerful than spears.

When the oil companies build roads into Waorani territory, outsiders, such as the Quichua and **settlers**, will have easy access to Waorani lands. The distant Ecuadoran government often does not enforce the laws designed to safeguard the protectorate. As a result, outsiders will hunt, fish, log, plant crops, and make their homes in the forests traditionally used only by the Waorani.

The land is the hope and the future of the Waorani. Without their forests, they will not survive as a people into the next century. Time is crucial to them now. If the forests are protected, the Waorani will have time to learn to adjust to the changes introduced into their community.

Like people everywhere, the Waorani want to control their

own lives. They want to decide whether their children will live in the forests as their parents and grandparents did before them.

Very few Waorani can speak any language other than their own. And in the Waorani tradition there are no leaders. But despite these obstacles, the Waorani are responding to the rapid changes affecting their way of life. For the first time in their history they have organized. Their group, ONHAE, has a president and a vice president. However, Waorani society still remains highly egalitarian. There are still no real leaders in their culture. Today, many Waorani believe that their children should learn to read, write, and speak other languages so that they can defend their land and way of life.

Traditionally, Waorani could spear intruders to ensure safety and isolation in the jungle. But today the best weapons are the voices of the people. Their voices tell of land that is physically and spiritually part of the people. And their voices are beginning to be heard beyond their forests.

CHAPTER TWO

HARVESTING THE JUNGLE

"Long, long ago the ancestors told this story. . . ."

THE ORIGIN OF CASSAVA

Long ago they had no cassava plants. There were none. The ancestors always had sweet potatoes, and in those days they lived on sweet potatoes; they had no cassava.

Just as we do now, someone went hunting, and as he searched for animal tracks, he saw a great many tapir footprints. "Why are there so many tapir tracks? I just can't figure it out. They are right there beside the river where there are plants growing that I have never seen before."

Still wondering about it, the Waorani left. Later, he decided to go again and see. "I wonder why there are so many tapir tracks," he thought. Then he saw that many tapirs lived beside the patch of plants.

Then a plant spoke to him. "Take me. Pull up my roots from the ground. Take me with you. When you carry me to the house, peel off my skin and cook the inside part of the root. Then eat it. I am a very delicious food. I am cassava."

Taking just one piece of the cassava root with him, the

Waorani cooked it and ate it all up. "It was very good," he decided. "Now I'm going to get more cassava." So he went again to get more.

"This is what you must do to me," the cassava plant said. "Break off my stalk. After you have chopped down some trees and cleared away the weeds, plant me and let me grow. When I grow, and you see I have leaves, don't take me yet. Wait until all the leaves are grown, then clear the weeds. When you see the cassava in the ground humps up the earth, dig up the cassava root. Take it and eat it. Eat it like that. Then plant me on other clearings farther and farther away. I'll grow, and you will live by eating me."

So the Waorani took the cassava, chopped down the trees, planted it, and it grew. He cleared the weeds. Then the cassava root formed. He dug up a little to see. It was still not fully developed. After some time passed the root became big. "That's what the cassava plant said. When it's like that, it's mature," the Waorani thought.

So he ate it. Then he called to the others, "Come see! I happily took the tapir's cassava." Later the tapir himself went to his cassava patch, and when he saw that they had taken every bit and that there were no cassava roots left, he protested, "It was my cassava!" And he cried.

GARDENING

Cassava, also called manioc, is the **staple** food of the Waorani. The people plant manioc in small gardens in the forest. First the women, men, and children clear the undergrowth with large heavy knives called machetes. Then the men chop down the trees, using steel axes. The people used to use sharpened stones and wooden knives. Now it takes only a few days to clear a garden.

The felled trees are laid across the garden patch. The decaying trunks and leaves nourish and protect the soil. They provide the nutrients for growth in the rain forest. Most rain-forest soils have few nutrients. Over millions of years, rainfall has **leached** minerals from the soil, washing them downward deep into the earth. Decaying plants act like a sponge: They hold minerals in place long enough for new plant roots to take them up and use them for growth.

The Waorani women plant manioc by poking the stalks into the ground among the clutter of tree trunks and leaves. Once planted the garden requires weeding, which is backbreaking, difficult work.

After planting one garden, the people move on to another area of the forest to plant again. The women carry manioc stalks to the other patches. In the course of a year the Waorani plant three or four gardens. As a result the gardens mature at different times. After nine months the first garden is ready to harvest. The Waorani return and the women pull the entire plants out of the ground. The stalks are saved to plant again, and the tubers, or roots, are eaten.

The first step in preparing a garden–chopping down the trees.

Ripe manioc roots can remain in the ground for many months without rotting, so there is no rush to return to the gardens. Sometimes the Waorani will return to an old garden after a year or two and still be able to harvest manioc.

A garden is usually less than one acre in size. After a harvest the Waorani wait 12 to 15 years before planting manioc in the same place again. This gives plants and trees a chance to grow, thus protecting the soil from **erosion** and ensuring that nutrients will be recycled.

The Waorani do, however, sometimes plant shrubs and trees in old garden plots. One such plant is the barbasco shrub. Its leaves are picked and crushed to remove the poisonous

Women and girls harvest manioc, or cassava, in one of the several gardens the Waorani plant during the course of a year.

sap. The sap is dumped into streams, where it stuns fish and makes them easy to catch.

Although manioc is their main crop, the Waorani also grow plantain (a kind of tropical banana), peanuts, and maize (corn).

EAT, DRINK, AND . . .

The Waorani prepare manioc in two ways. Sometimes they peel the tubers and then boil them with meat. Boiled manioc tubers are similar to boiled potatoes.

But usually the manioc is boiled and mashed into a paste. Water is added to make a thick drink called *tepae*. While stirring the *tepae* with a wooden spoon, the women chew mouthfuls of mash and then spit it back into the pot. The **enzymes** from their saliva cause the mash to ferment, or become slightly alcoholic, within a few days. But the Waorani let it ferment only overnight so that it is very weak and not intoxicating.

When the Waorani drink the *tepae*, they dilute it with three times as much water. The Waorani enjoy *tepae* throughout the day, all year long. *Tepae* is so important to the Waorani that in their language the word for happiness means literally "another bowl of *tepae*."

. . . BE MERRY!

Tepae can also be made from other fruit, such as bananas and peach palm, also called chonta fruit. Red chonta fruits grow in

Women prepare tepae, the thick manioc drink that the people love.

bunches about 60 feet above the ground. But the bark of the chonta tree is covered with sharp spines, making climbing impossible. The Waorani plant smooth-barked trees next to the chonta and use them for climbing.

Tree climbing is a difficult yet essential skill learned by children at a young age. Most rain-forest trees do not have branches on the lower part of the trunk. A tree may shoot 75 feet into the sky before branches emerge to form part of the rain-forest **canopy**.

Waorani climb trees by tying their feet together with vines

and wrapping their ankles around the base of a tree. Then they pull their bodies up with their arms and pull and push their feet up the tree. Sometimes they transfer from a smaller tree to a larger tree 50 or 60 feet above the ground. Sixty feet above the ground they let go of the tree with their hands and poke at the chonta fruit with a long pole. Their knees and feet grip the tree until they are ready to slide down.

In the tropical rain forest, which lies close to the equator, there is no summer or winter season. But between January and April more fruit ripens than at any other time of the year. These months are called the chonta season because the fruit of the chonta tree is ripe and plentiful.

The people enjoy the abundance of the chonta fruit, which they make into *tepae*. During the chonta season the people travel throughout the forest visiting friends and relatives. They celebrate all night long, singing, dancing, and drinking bowls and bowls of *tepae*.

The months following the chonta season are called the fat season. This is the time when monkeys are fat from eating fruit. During the fat season monkeys are hunted a great deal.

WILD FOODS

Plants that grow wild in the jungle are also part of the Waorani "garden." The Waorani have learned which wild plants are good to eat. While out hunting or walking to and from gardens, the

A Waorani transfers from one tree to another in search of fruit, birds' eggs, and monkeys. It's a dangerous feat, one that takes great skill and endurance.

Children share the wild honey they found in the forest.

Waorani often pick and eat berries and fruit along the way. Sometimes they quickly weave baskets out of palm fronds to fill with fruit for the rest of the people in the village.

The discovery of a beehive is a joyful occasion. Honey is a fairly rare treat, and the Waorani will make great efforts to get it. Honey, berries, and fruit provide the Waorani with important minerals and vitamins needed for good health. Although cultivated and wild plants provide the Waorani with most of their calories, they also depend on wild **game** for protein.

HUNTERS

In the Waorani culture the women plant and harvest the gardens, and the men hunt. Both activities are equally important and essential for survival.

Men go out hunting once or twice a week. Usually a man goes alone or with one other man. Occasionally a group of men will go together, but there is never a leader.

Hunting is an intense and demanding pursuit. There are real dangers, such as snakebites and puncture wounds from stepping on slashed saplings. A hunter often travels many miles before reaching a good area, and he must carry his game home on his back. When a hunter returns from the jungle, he is tired but filled with a sense of achievement, adventure, and joy. While the women prepare the meat over the fire, he tells his story of the hunt. He describes the pursuit, the weapons he used, and adds the small details that make each hunting experience different.

Hunters use wooden spears to kill peccary, or wild pigs, which roam the forests. Spears are made out of chonta wood and are about 12 feet long. Brightly colored feathers and grips made from woven vines help a hunter pick out his own spear from someone else's.

Spear hunting provides only a small amount of meat for the Waorani, however. Most of the animals in the rain forest live more than 100 feet above the ground, high in the forest canopy. Out of a spear's reach and out of a person's sight, monkeys and birds seem like impossible targets. But the Waorani have developed the perfect rain-forest weapon.

THE BLOWGUN

The blowgun is an ancient weapon used to kill monkeys and birds. A hunter blows air from his lungs into his blowgun to fire poison darts high into the canopy.

Usually a hunter remains on the ground. Rarely, he climbs a tree to get closer to his **prey**. Often he first locates his target by the sounds he hears above his head.

The construction of a blowgun and poison darts requires great skill. The Waorani make them using only materials that grow in the forest. The entire process takes about two weeks.

The gun itself is made from a ten-foot-long piece of chonta wood that has been separated into two halves. The barrel is made by cutting a quarter-inch groove along the center of each piece. Then the pieces are fitted and bound together with vines. The inside of the barrel is finished to a smooth surface by pushing sand through it with a long stick. During the last stages of sanding, fine clay is used instead of sand to make the barrel silky smooth.

POISON ARROWS

The darts fired from Waorani blowguns are made out of palm-frond stems splintered into 18-inch-long pieces. The sharp tips are dipped into a deadly poison called **curare** (kyoo-RAR-ee). When a poison dart pierces the skin of an animal, the prey is paralyzed and dies quickly. Small birds and animals die instantly,

A hunter uses his blowgun to kill birds and monkeys high in the treetops.

but larger prey, such as a howler monkey, may require several darts and take up to 20 minutes to fall from the trees.

Curare is made from the bark of the curare vine. Bark is placed into a cone of leaves and water is dripped over it. The water filters through the bark and the leaf cone into a bowl. Then the liquid is boiled over the fire to concentrate the curare into a black paste. The dart tips are dipped into the paste and dried near the fire. The tips remain sticky, and care is taken to keep the darts from touching one another. The hunter places them in a bamboo holder, which he wears slung from his neck.

BLOWGUN HUNTING

Darts need to be "feathered" in order to work. **Feathering** is made out of kapok, a white cottonlike fiber that surrounds the seeds of the kapok tree. Feathering keeps a dart moving in a straight line. It is also essential for making a tight seal inside the blowgun barrel. When the hunter blows, the feathering allows enough air pressure to build behind the dart to launch it 100 feet into the canopy.

Hunters collect kapok fiber and store it in gourds, the dried shells of certain fruits. The fiber-filled gourd is carried around the hunter's neck within quick and easy reach.

Before firing a blowgun, a hunter winds some kapok fiber around the base of a dart. He pushes the dart into the barrel of the gun, poisoned tip first. He raises the gun to his mouth, seals

Birds like these wire-tailed manakins are shot for their bright feathers, which are used to decorate headdresses, armbands, and spears.

his lips against the barrel, and blows. Pressure builds in his lungs as air is forced against the feathered dart.

Then, in an explosion of force, the dart breaks away, speeding through the polished gun barrel and into the sky. The entire process–feathering the dart, placing it in the gun, taking aim, and blowing–takes just seconds. More than 100 darts may be used in a single hunt.

Sometimes a hunter climbs a tree to get closer to his target. His feet bound with vines and his knees gripping the tree, he arches his back, throws back his head, and raises the gun to his mouth. The skills and strength needed to hunt with a blowgun are equal to those of an Olympic athlete.

Hunters return to their villages with dead woolly, spider, and howler monkeys. The birds they take include parrots, macaws, guans, and curassows. As in many cultures, the Waorani have **taboos** against eating certain kinds of animals or birds. They never eat birds of prey, such as the harpy eagle, or snakes, and they do not like deer meat–they say that deer eyes look too human.

The women prepare monkeys for cooking by first burning off the fur in the fire. Then they gut, or clean, them before cutting them up. Birds are plucked of their feathers. Most meat is boiled in a pot, although sometimes a pig or monkey is roasted above the fire.

THE "GARDEN"

Until recently, most non-native people have thought of the Amazon rain forest as a cruel and frightening place–a green hell. They were intruders in the forest and did not understand how to survive in it. They sought to conquer and tame the jungle.

Today many outsiders like to think of the rain forest as a gentle and beautiful place–a Garden of Eden. These people ignore the jungle's often harsh realities.

To the Waorani, their forests are neither a green hell nor

a Garden of Eden. Challenging and often difficult, life in the rain forest may not be paradise. But the rain forest *is* a kind of garden–a garden that can be harvested only with knowledge, cooperation, respect, and strength.

CHAPTER THREE

LIFE IN THE RAIN FOREST

THE RAINBOW

The ancestors said, "When you see the rainbow in the distance, look there and you will find the place where the good clay pits are."

Then they said, "Don't point at the rainbow. If you point at it your arm will become paralyzed. Just nod with your head.

"Up there is the rainbow, look over there. Be sure you never point with your hand. Then, wherever the rainbow touches the earth, quickly go to that place. The clay you find there will surely be the best clay for making pots. Go there and search, and search, and search. Bring back the clay."

And when the Waorani found the clay they said, "This is excellent clay!" Then they used it to make good clay pots.

Traditionally the Waorani made all their pots from clay. Today metal pots are replacing clay pots because they are lightweight and don't break. Indeed the Waorani have obtained many items such as knives, axes, and even clothing and boots, that are helpful with daily life in the rain forest.

However, most of the items needed and used by the Waorani are still fashioned from the materials found in the rain forest. The blowgun, for example, is better than the shotgun for hunting animals and birds in the canopy. And the skills and knowledge needed to make these things are found among the people, especially the **elders**. Now, as in the past, Waorani children learn their unique way of life from their parents and grandparents.

THE YOUNGEST WAORANI

In the Waorani culture children call many women "mother" and many men "father." A child calls all of her mother's sisters *waana,* or mother. And all of her father's brothers are *waempo,* or father. But just one mother–the woman who gives birth to the baby–provides the infant with the loving care needed for a healthy start in life.

Waorani babies come into the world quietly. A young mother does little to prepare for her new baby. Usually her mother helps deliver the baby onto a "sheet" of fresh banana leaves. If the baby is a girl, the grandmother names her. Boys are named by their grandfathers. The next day the new mother will probably be in her manioc garden, working as she does every other day. And her new baby will be with her.

Waorani babies are in the constant care of their mothers. They are carried in baby slings until they are at least two years old. At night they sleep in their mother's hammock. They nurse until they are three or four years old.

Babies do not wear diapers or any other clothing. They are simply cradled in the soft bark that has been peeled from a fig tree and made into a baby sling. The sling is worn over the mother's shoulder and the baby rests comfortably on her hip or against her chest. When the sling is soiled, it is easily washed–along with the baby. Babies are kept clean by several daily baths in shallow streams.

Traditionally, no one in the Waorani culture wore clothing. The only item worn was a G-string, or **komi**, around the waist. Today many Waorani wear clothes when convenient or available. However, these Waorani still wear their *komis* underneath their clothes. If a person does not have a *komi,* he or she is considered nude.

The Waorani are offended by outsiders or tourists who swim or bathe in the nude. Their definition of nudity simply differs from ours.

GROWING, LEARNING

A child is no longer carried in the baby sling when he or she can walk through the forest between the manioc gardens. Now the jungle is a playground to explore. Children don't have toys, except for sticks, leaves, and animals found in the forest. Boys and girls climb trees, splash in streams, slide down muddy riverbanks, collect and eat berries, fish, hunt, play "ball" with old insect nests, and wrestle. Games are just for fun—there is never a winner or loser.

By the time a boy is nine years old, he knows how to use his father's blowgun. At first he hunts with darts that haven't been dipped in poison. His prey are small birds and animals. When he is 16, a young man is strong and coordinated enough to hunt for large monkeys and birds.

Children eat when they are hungry and do not live by a schedule. If a boy catches a small fish or bird, his mother will cook it for him to eat. At night children go to bed when they're tired. They are often lulled to sleep by the voices of their parents and other adults talking and telling stories. Children sleep in hammocks with two or three of their brothers, sisters, or friends. During the chonta season, when the people stay up all night singing, dancing, and drinking *tepae*, children stay awake, too.

Children are not formally taught how to do things, yet they learn everything they need to know by playing and watching. For example, most eight-year-olds know how to start a fire—an important skill. They place kapok fibers under a soft log and then twirl a hard stick into the log. They keep twirling until small embers are created, which light the kapok and get the fire going.

To avoid getting sore hands every time fire is needed, the

Relaxing at home in the evening, Waorani enjoy telling stories, singing, and joking.

Waorani keep their fires going day and night. When walking between gardens, they carry the smoldering fire in a termite nest.

PETS

Children learn the feeding habits, cries, calls, and smells of wild animals and birds by keeping many pets. Sometimes a mother monkey is shot on a hunting trip. The baby found clinging to her fur becomes a pet for the children. Birds are tied with vines to poles and kept inside the huts. Sometimes parrots are taught to mimic people, screeching Waorani phrases into the jungle as the people walk between their gardens.

Young Waorani learn how to start a fire. It takes a long time to get the flame going, so the people have an important rule: Never let the fire go out.

Pets are fun to keep, but they are also an important way to learn about animals and birds. A hunter can identify and locate a bird or animal without ever seeing it. Its call, the sounds it makes while moving, and even the smell of its urine dripping from the canopy tell a hunter what **species** is above.

MARRIAGE

Almost without knowing it, a child grows into an adult. No birthdays have been celebrated because the Waorani do not keep track of age. There have been no graduations or celebrations marking achievements. Yet a young adult knows how to do everything to make a good life in the rain forest.

When a young person is between 14 and 18 years old, he or she may be ready for marriage. In the Waorani culture people do not fall in love and get married. Instead marriages are arranged by parents and grandparents. Often a woman may have two husbands or a man may have two wives.

There are special rules about who a young person may marry. "Cross cousins" may marry each other, but marriage between other cousins is forbidden. Cross cousins are the sons and daughters of aunts and uncles. Aunts are sisters of a child's father. Uncles are brothers of a child's mother.

Children consider all of their mother's sisters their mother and all of their father's brothers their father. These "mothers" and "fathers" are not considered aunts and uncles, and therefore, their children are not considered cousins, but brothers and sisters. And, of course, marriage between brothers and sisters is forbidden. There are so few Waorani that actually everyone is fairly closely related.

Marriage is a working partnership. Both men and women have specific roles that ensure that the entire group will survive. Marriage also binds groups of Waorani together. This **kinship** forms the strong ties that make everyone part of a larger family group.

When a young couple marries, they are often taken by surprise. Although young people may suspect who their spouse

A grandmother displays her pet monkey. The large holes in her earlobes used to be considered the mark of a true Waorani. Today, however, young people no longer practice this tradition.

will be, they do not know for sure. And they do not know when the marriage will take place.

During a *tepae* drinking celebration a young man may be brought to the hut of his new bride. The couple is pushed into a hammock and the two feed each other *tepae*, in much the same way American newlyweds feed each other wedding cake.

The people sing a marriage song and sometimes an elder gives advice. All night long the people sing and dance. Beginning the next day the young couple will live together with the girl's parents.

HUTS AND HAMMOCKS

Sometimes a young couple will build their own hut after their first child is born. The men do most of the construction. First they chop down several tall, slender trees for the poles that will provide the frame for the hut. The poles are tied together with vines to form a large rectangle about 30 feet long and 15 feet wide. A triangular-shaped arch is built over the rectangle to make a gently sloping roof.

The roof is made of two layers: an outer layer of palm fronds and an inner layer of palm leaves. A large hut requires about 4,000 leaves and 40 giant palm fronds. The smaller, traditional style uses far fewer leaves. Both styles provide protection from heavy rains and the hot sun.

A hut lasts for barely a year before it becomes infested with insects. The Waorani usually burn down old huts when they leave for another area of the forest. Insects are killed by the fire. It is important to eliminate the insects so that a hut can be built in the same place sometime in the future.

It takes about five days to build a hut. Machetes and steel axes have made the job much easier than it was before such tools were available. But making the "furniture" used inside the hut is a different story.

Constructing a hut. The roof is covered with an outer layer of palm fronds and an inner layer of palm leaves.

Hammocks are the only "furniture" used by the Waorani. Made by the women, they last for only one or two years but require many hours of labor. It takes about three months to make one hammock, and many hammocks are needed–so women are always making them, year-round.

Hammocks are woven out of the fiber stripped from the inside of young palm stems. This fiber, called raffia, is dried and then spun into a very long string by rolling it against the thigh. The string, which is about a mile long, is woven on a square wooden frame to make the hammock.

Finished hammocks are very strong and can hold up to five

Girls learn how to weave at an early age. These girls are making string bags, which they will sell to tourists.

people. But every adult has his or her own, and the children share hammocks, sleeping two or three together.

A BIG FAMILY

The Waorani live in a community where everyone can do everything. There are no separate farmers, gun makers, hunters, or house builders. Together, each husband and wife can do everything to make a living in the rain forest. And by sharing among one another, the Waorani always have enough of everything. When a hunter brings game back to the community, he divides it up equally with all the people.

The women work together, making hammocks, preparing *tepae*, gardening, cooking, and caring for children. Although they are usually busy with some kind of work, they are together, talking and sharing stories.

During the heat of the afternoon the Waorani sometimes rest in their huts. Swinging in their hammocks, the people have time to spend with their friends and family.

At the end of each day the Waorani groom one another by removing insects from skin and hair. Grooming is essential in the rain-forest environment because many insects try to attach themselves to people's skin. Some of the annoying pests are **parasites**, which can cause disease. People enjoy grooming. Not only is it important for good health, but it is also comforting and gives the people a feeling of closeness.

Boys groom one another to remove rain-forest insects from their hair and skin.

GROWING OLDER

The Waorani are a healthy people. Daily physical labor combined with a balanced diet of fresh food and pure water has reduced the threat of disease. In Waorani society there is no cancer, high blood pressure, or heart disease.

But the Waorani are not free from all health-related problems. Most obvious is tooth decay. Lice and fungal infections are very common in the rain forest and are difficult to get rid of.

Recently some Waorani have gotten ill or died from diseases carried by outsiders. Polio, measles, pneumonia, and flu are diseases to which the Waorani have no natural resistance. In

1968, 16 Waorani died from polio, which was introduced through contact with Quichua. Today most Waorani have been **immunized** against many diseases.

Illness accounts for a relatively small number of deaths–about 10 percent. Snakebites and accidents, such as falling from trees, are the main causes of death today. The Waorani have the highest rate of death from snakebites on earth. Hunting game in the canopy requires that a hunter look up as he walks through the forest. Sometimes he steps too close to a poisonous snake and cannot escape its deadly bite.

In the past more Waorani died from spearing raids by other Waorani than from any other cause. In fact, more than 40 percent of all Waorani died in spear attacks. Today most Waorani are living long lives and simply dying of old age. Some are believed to be in their 70s. It is still too early, however, to predict what the average life span of the Waorani will be.

JUNGLE MEDICINE

Compared to many tribes in Amazonia, the Waorani use relatively few plants, about 35 species, to treat illness. Some scientists think the Waorani had little need to experiment with a wide variety of plants because they were not exposed to European diseases until the mid-20th century, when cures, vaccines, and treatments were already available. In contrast, other native tribes in South America were exposed to Europeans much earlier, beginning with the Spanish in the 15th century. The epidemics carried from Europe wiped out millions of indigenous people and forced the remaining natives to look for treatments and cures among their plants.

When Waorani are injured or get sick, they treat themselves with a variety of medicines made from tropical plants. The medicines are prepared to treat injuries or symptoms of diseases, such as fever, rashes, infections, aches, and swelling. Sometimes a plant with a bad smell is used to force a fever out of the body. The Waorani believe that the properties of a plant, in this case bad smell, can be passed to the sick person, causing the illness to leave the body.

Traditional Waorani medicine is different from medicine practiced by doctors in modern industrial societies. **Western medicine** seeks to understand and treat the causes of disease. In contrast, the Waorani often do not know what has caused an illness. They rely instead on remedies to relieve only symptoms.

Certain illnesses in the jungle, however, cannot be treated by herbal medicines alone. These afflictions, the Waorani believe, are caused by spirits, or *wenae,* and they must be treated by the **shaman**. The shaman is a healer who is thought to have power to cure illnesses caused by spirits.

These spirits have been sent by the shaman himself–or herself–to live inside the body, and only the shaman can banish them. The shaman uses a hallucinogenic, or mind-altering, medicine made from a plant to drive the spirit away.

RITUALS AND CELEBRATIONS

Unlike many indigenous people, the Waorani practice few **rituals**. Rituals are certain fixed forms of ceremonies. People practice them in hopes of having their wishes granted.

Sometimes a Waorani father may slap his son's back with stinging nettles; this is supposed to make the boy grow into a strong and good hunter. In another ritual the hands of children are slapped against the cheeks of a dead pig. This will make the girls plant manioc that will "grow as big as pigs," and boys will grow to be as "fast and active as pigs." In another ritual hunters dip their darts into curare smeared on the side of a clay pot used for cooking monkey meat. It is believed that darts prepared in this way will have the power to seek out prey. As he prepares his darts, the hunter sings a hunting song.

More common than rituals are *aemae,* or celebrations during the chonta season. The people prepare for *aemae* by painting their bodies and faces with dyes made from plants, berries, and charcoal. The traditional design for men is a black back with zigzags and dots painted on the arms. Everyone wears headbands and arm bands woven out of raffia. Bright feathers from macaws, harpy eagles, toucans, and other rain-forest birds are laced into the bands.

Aemae are important to the Waorani because the

A father slaps his son with stinging nettles. The people believe that this ritual will help pass along the father's hunting abilities to his son.

Young boys have traditional designs painted on their bodies in anticipation of aemae, the celebrations held during the chonta fruit season.

All dressed up for aemae. *Children and parents alike look forward to the festivities that bring people together.*

celebrations bring people together from distant parts of the forest. They share news and stories and renew family ties. They share the abundance of food that the forest has provided. And they express themselves in singing and dancing.

The people dance with hands on the shoulders of the person in front of them. They sing songs that sound like chants. Many of the songs are about hunting, chopping down trees to plant gardens, and sharing meat among everyone. The songs express the ancient and deep emotions felt by people who live close together generation after generation.

CHAPTER FOUR

THE GLOBAL VILLAGE

"This story was told long, long ago by the ancient ones whenever they ate corn. . . ."

THE ORIGIN OF THE CORN BEES

Once some Waorani had a lot of corn. A man asked, "Can I have some of your corn to eat?" But the Waorani refused to give it to him.

So the man chopped down the forest to make a cornfield. He made a great big field for corn. He planted some corn. So much corn grew that it was like cane in a cane patch.

Then the Waorani said to the man, "When your corn is grown, and we see it is ripe and that you are eating it, let us eat it, too."

But the man replied, "Since you refused to share with me and ate all your corn, I refuse, too. When the corn is ripe, all alone I will eat it up. In one day I am going to gobble it all up."

Then one day the corn tassels became dark. When the tassels became dark, the man ate all his corn in one day! The scoundrel! He piled firewood high on the ground-fire and cooked all the corn, every bit of it. He acted as if he had been starved.

He ate so much corn that his abdomen suddenly swelled

and burst open. All the corn spilled out of his stomach and spread all over the ground. And around that place, the corn bees buzzed and buzzed.

"The Origin of the Corn Bees" is a story about a man who wanted corn. He worked hard to get the corn and then he ate so much that his stomach exploded. Perhaps the Waorani tell the story simply to explain where corn bees came from.

But when others hear the story, they may be reminded of someone they know who eats too much–a glutton. The story seems to be warning people not to be selfish, but to share what they have with others. The man in the story may also be understood as a symbol of a larger group of people–such as a country–that uses too many of the earth's resources.

GLUTTONS AND GUZZLERS?

The United States uses 40 percent of the world's supply of gasoline. And 49 percent of the oil drilled in Ecuador is shipped to the United States. Yet the United States has less than 5 percent of the world's people.

In 1992 the first world meeting on the environment, known as Earth Summit, was held in Brazil. The **third world**, or developing countries, voiced its message: It's time for the rich, industrialized countries to reduce their consumption of the world's resources. This overconsumption is responsible for many problems, such

Preparing the chonta fruit for all to share. Waorani are taught at an early age that in order to survive they must share the resources of the forest.

as the destruction of the **ozone layer**.

Perhaps the biggest challenge for the 21st century is the need to create a more balanced world, where resources are shared more fairly among all people. But the creation of a balanced world will not be accomplished easily. The way people think about the earth is firmly rooted in history. Five hundred years ago, European explorers began to travel to faraway places in search of riches–gold, spices, silk, animal furs, and slaves. The merchants and traders who bought and sold material goods and slaves became wealthy. Today a similar kind of **colonialism** continues. Countries from the developed, or industrialized, world still look to poorer nations for resources.

WEALTH OF THE LAND

How do you define wealth? If you're like a lot of people, wealth means having lots of money, or owning land or resources that can be sold. But if you ask a Waorani child if she is rich or poor, she probably won't know what you mean.

In the traditional Waorani culture there is no currency, or money. People do not buy or sell anything. Instead the land provides them with food, water, and shelter. Although the Waorani have no money, they are not poor. The rain forest and the traditions passed from generation to generation provide the people with everything they need. The knowledge, skills, and kinship that come with living in their culture cannot be measured in money.

Today, the land of the Waorani is threatened by the search for oil. Oil exploration and drilling are dangerous to the Waorani in many complicated ways. Oil is poisonous and pollutes the land and rivers when it is taken out of the earth. During oil exploration, explosions echo through the forests, disturbing animals and birds, causing them to run away and leave behind their young.

The land provides the Waorani with everything they need–including a plentiful supply of fish.

Clearing the forests for exploration and drilling also destroys the land. Without the trees, precious soil is lost and toxic chemicals are washed into streams, destroying fish and making the water unfit for drinking. Also, oil workers carry foreign diseases, which can infect the indigenous people.

Perhaps more dangerous than anything else are the roads that are built deep into the forest so that pipelines can be constructed and oil rigs maintained by crews of workers. Following the workers are outsiders, who will use the resources of the forests: Quichua who hunt and fish, settlers who plant **cash crops**, loggers who take timber, miners who search for minerals, and tourists who come to see and experience the rain forest.

Some scientists think oil exploration and development is going to happen no matter how much people protest against it. These experts say that if roads could be sealed off to outsiders, then the Waorani might actually benefit from the **royalty** money oil drilling would produce. This money could be used for the health care and education that would be needed as more Waorani come into contact with outsiders. But others argue that once the roads are built, it will be almost impossible to keep outsiders from entering Waorani lands.

In a perfect world the Waorani would be the people to decide the future of their ancestral lands. Although the voices of the Waorani are beginning to be heard, they must compete with powerful forces beyond their borders.

Tourists, without meaning to, pose a great threat to the Waorani. They may transmit diseases to which the Waorani have no resistance.

MANY VISIONS

The battle for the Ecuadoran rain forests involves several groups of people, each with their own special interests. Those favoring

65

oil drilling include the people who control the government of Ecuador. They seek to benefit from the profits to be made from the oil and they hope to improve the economy of Ecuador.

The people who own the oil companies also, of course, want to profit from sales. Petroecuador, the government-owned oil company, and foreign companies such as Texaco, Gulf, Conoco, BP, Arco, and Maxus Energy Corporation all have an interest in the Oriente.

Another group, in sharp contrast to the first two, is made up of the ordinary, poor people of Ecuador. They lack basic things: clean water, sufficient food, adequate housing. They want jobs and land for ranching or farming. Oil drilling could provide the jobs, and the roads could pave the way into the rain-forest "frontier."

Standing against these powerful forces are the **environmentalists**. They want to protect the rain forests because they are **biologically diverse**. Millions of different kinds of plants, insects, and animals inhabit the forests–most of these species have yet to be discovered and named. If the forests are destroyed, many of these species will become extinct.

What is most important: the economy of Ecuador, the oil for the industrial world, the landless poor in Ecuador, the rich rain-forest environment, or the Waorani?

TRIBAL WISDOM

The wisdom that tribal peoples have passed down from generation to generation is now being recognized as a valuable re-source. Their knowledge of plant and animal life is far more detailed than information available to specially trained tropical ecologists. This knowledge could be important to the rest of the world. Many scientists recognize that it will be lost if the Waorani are forced from their land.

More important, however, than specific knowledge about plants, animals, or the environment are values. Respect for people and other living things, cooperation and sharing, and tolerance and acceptance of each individual are the values that help several Waorani families live together in one palm-thatched hut.

The world today is like a large village of huts. Inside the huts are people of different languages, customs, and traditions. Yet all the people have similar needs–clean water and air, food, and the freedom to live in the ways they have inherited or chosen. Perhaps the needs of all can be better satisfied if our **global village** adopts some of the values held by the Waorani and other tribal peoples.

ACTIVITIES

1. Draw pictures to illustrate one or more of the stories told by the Waorani. You will need several pieces of paper; a pencil, colored pencils, markers, or crayons; and reference books or field guides showing animals that live in Amazonia (find these in the library).

When you have finished, try telling the story to a friend or relative. Use the pictures to help you remember what happens in the story.

2. Make a small guidebook showing some of the plants and animals used by the Waorani. Below is a list of the plants and animals mentioned or discussed in this book. Make a guide with the following materials: 20-30 large index cards, pen, hole punch, yarn or string, and crayons or markers. You will need reference books such as *A Neotropical Companion*, by John C. Kricher (Princeton University Press, 1989) to help you learn about the plants and animals to be included in the guide. (Ask your librarian to help you find other references that include information and pictures.)

PLANTS

barbasco shrub	maize	peanut
curare vine	manioc (cassava)	plantain
fig tree	palm tree	sweet potato
kapok tree	peach palm (chonta tree)	

ANIMALS

bees	howler monkey	spider monkey
curassow	macaw	tapir
guan	parrot	toucan
harpy eagle	peccary	woolly monkey

Make the guide by drawing a picture of the plant or animal on the blank side of the index card. On the ruled side include the following information:

- name of plant or animal
- genus and species (the plant's or animal's scientific name)
- range (the geographic area in which the species lives)
- habitat (the kind of surroundings the species requires)
- food the animal eats
- interesting characteristics (such as sounds or coloring)
- uses by Waorani (food, tools, shelter, dyes)

Make a cover card for the guidebook. A possible title for the book could be "Some Plants and Animals Used by the Waorani Indians of Ecuador." When all the cards are completed, stack them together and use the hole punch to make one or more holes along one edge. Loop the yarn through the holes to bind the cards together. Share your guidebook with classmates, teachers, and relatives.

3. <u>Create a poster showing one day in the life of a Waorani child.</u> You could include activities described in chapter 3. Use your imagination to create scenes such as games with other children, starting a fire, hunting, cooking, grooming, or resting in hammocks inside a hut. You will need a piece of poster board; markers, crayons, or paints; brushes; and pieces of sponge (to dab in paint and use to print leaves). Write a few paragraphs that explain each scene in the poster.

4. <u>Visit a museum to see and learn about the tools used by South American Indians.</u> Many museums display pottery, spears, blowguns, knives, baskets, and other items made by tribal peoples of South

America. Compare these items to those used by the Waorani. What are the similarities and differences?

5. <u>Learn more about your own culture.</u> Talk with a grandparent or other older relative to learn more about the culture of which your family is a part. You could write down some of the things you learn, or use a tape recorder to interview the person. If possible, look through an old photo album with your relative. Ask him or her to explain the pictures. When you have learned a few new things, write a short story about your family and your culture.

Here are some questions you could ask: What are some of the ceremonies, traditions, customs, and rituals your family observes? What are the origins of these traditions? Are there special clothes or hats worn during any of the ceremonies? What are the meanings behind some of the ceremonies? Does your culture have a ritual that marks the change from a child into an adult? What are some of the traditional foods prepared?

6. <u>Learn about organizations working to defend the rights of the Waorani and other indigenous peoples around the world.</u> Survival International is one whose mission is to help protect the lands and cultures of tribal people. Write to learn more about its activities and how you can become involved.

> Survival International
> 310 Edgeware Road
> London W2 1DY
> United Kingdom

Survival International has a special membership category for young people called Young Survival. If you join, you will receive an Action Pack that explains how you can "walk your talk," or *do* things rather than just talk about them.

Cultural Survival
215 First Street
Cambridge, MA 02142

or

Cultural Survival (Canada)
Suite 420
1 Nicholas Street
Ottawa, Ontario K1N 7B7
Canada

7. Write letters to protest oil drilling in Ecuador's Oriente. When you write, be polite and use the following guide to help you make your points. Write the letters to be sent to Ecuador in Spanish if you know how.

a. State that you are very concerned about oil exploration and drilling in the Oriente and the damage caused to the Waorani and the forests.

b. The Waorani should have the right to choose their own future. They should be given legal rights to all their territory.

c. The government should stop settlers from traveling into Waorani lands along roads built by oil companies.

d. Young Waorani should be able to live in the culture given to them by their parents. (You could mention that you are a young person, too.)

Send your letters to government officials in Ecuador and to the oil company listed below.

President of the
Republic of Ecuador
Garcia Moreno 1043
Quito, Ecuador

Executive Director IERAC
Instituto Ecuadororiano Reforma
    Agraria y Colonisacion
Carrion 1040
Quito, Ecuador

Public Relations Director
Maxus Exploration Company
717 North Harwood Street
Dallas, TX 75201

8. <u>Write letters to your elected officials and urge them to make energy conservation a priority in the United States.</u> Use the following guide to make your points. Be polite and tell them that you are a young person concerned about the future.

   a. The United States uses 40 percent of the world's supply of gasoline although it has less than 5 percent of the people.

   b. Most of the oil we use is to fuel cars. Many cars get poor gas mileage. Laws could be passed to require that cars get better mileage.

   c. Education about energy conservation should be an important priority.

   d. The government should give more support to the development of public transportation and clean-energy alternatives.

   e. Oil exploration and drilling in foreign countries, such as in Ecuador, is destroying traditional cultures, such as that of the Waorani.

Address your letters to the following officials:

   The Honorable (name of the president)
   President of the United States
   The White House
   Washington, DC 20500

   The Honorable (name of representative)
   United States House of Representatives
   Washington, DC 20515

   The Honorable (name of senator)
   United States Senate
   Washington, DC 20510

GLOSSARY

aemae–Waorani word for "celebration."

anthropologist–a person who studies people, including physical and cultural characteristics, customs, and social relationships.

biologically diverse–having a variety of plant and animal species in a given area.

canopy–the top layer of tree growth in the rain forest, which is about 100 feet above the ground.

cash crops–crops that are grown to be sold for profit; usually grown on large plantations.

colonialism–the system by which a country enters a foreign land in order to make a profit from exploiting, or using, the resources found there.

cowodi–Waorani word for "outsider."

culture–the complete way of living–including ideas, customs, skills, and arts–of a people.

curare–a black, sticky substance made from the juices extracted from the bark of certain South American vines and used by some indigenous people for poisoning the tips of arrows.

egalitarian–the belief that all people in a community should have equal political, social, and economic rights.

elder–an older person with authority and dignity within a community.

environmentalists–people concerned about the earth and who work to solve problems such as pollution.

enzymes–chemicals in saliva that start the digestive process.

erosion–the washing away of soil by rain or wind. This happens when there are no trees or plants to hold soil in place.

THE WAORANI

feathering–cottonlike fiber used on the ends of arrows during blowgun hunting.

fossils–hardened remains or traces of plant or animal life of some previous geological time.

game–wild birds or animals hunted for food or sport.

global village–the modern world, in which all peoples are closely connected and are interdependent.

immunized–to be given an inoculation or shot that protects a person from a specific disease.

indigenous–people who belong, or have traditionally lived, in an area; also called native, tribal, original, aboriginal, or first people.

kinship–close relationships between members of a family.

komi–Waorani word for the G-string worn around the waist.

leach–to dissolve minerals out of soil by the action of rainfall.

missionaries–people who are sent by their church to a foreign country to preach, teach, and convert indigenous people to their religious faith.

ozone layer–a layer of gas in the atmosphere that prevents the sun's dangerous ultraviolet radiation from reaching the earth.

parasite–a plant or animal that lives on or in another species, called a host; usually parasites harm their hosts, causing diseases.

prey–an animal hunted or killed for food.

rituals–ceremonies, rites, or religious observances practiced by a culture.

royalty–a share of the profits from oil or minerals taken from the land.

rubber gatherers–people who harvest latex by tapping rubber trees in the rain forest.

settlers–people who move to the rain forest from another area and try to grow crops or raise cattle.

shaman–a priest who cures diseases by using supernatural powers to banish evil spirits from the body; also called a "medicine man."

species–a group of animals or plants that are alike in several ways.

staple–the most important food or material that is made, grown, or sold in a region.

taboo–anything that is forbidden by tradition.

tepae–Waorani word for a thick drink made from crushed and fermented manioc tubers or chonta fruit.

third world–the "developing" countries of the world, where most of the people do not have access to modern consumer goods such as appliances, cars, and televisions; most of the people in third-world countries are poor and have inadequate water, food, and housing.

western medicine–the system of medicine that seeks to understand and treat the causes of disease; this system contrasts with traditional medicine, such as that practiced by indigenous groups, which treats the symptoms, rather than the causes, of diseases.

SELECTED BIBLIOGRAPHY

BOOKS

Broennimann, Peter. *Auca on the Cononaco*. Basel, Switzerland: Birkhauser Verlag Basel. 1981.

Collins, Mark, ed. *The Last Rain Forests*. New York: Oxford University Press. 1990.

Elliot, Elisabeth. *Through Gates of Splendor*. New York: Harper and Brothers Publishers. 1957.

Grennio, Angela, ed. *Amazonia: Voices from the Rainforest*. San Francisco: Rainforest Action Network. 1990.

Hames, Raymond B. and William T. Vickers, eds. *Adaptive Responses of Native Amazonians*. New York: Academic Press. 1983.

Kimerling, Judith. *Amazon Crude*. Natural Resources Defense Council. 1991.

Man, Jon. *Jungle Nomads of Ecuador: The Waorani*. London: Time-Life Books. 1982.

Pike, Evelyn G. and Rachel Saint, eds. *Workpapers Concerning Waorani Discourse Features*. Dallas: Summer Institute of Linguistics, Inc. 1988.

Whitten, Norman E. Jr., ed. *Cultural Transformations and Ethnicity in Modern Ecuador*. Champaign-Urbana: University of Illinois Press. 1981.

JOURNALS

Cooper, Marc. "Rain Forest Crude." *Mother Jones*. March/April 1992.

Davis, E. Wade and James A. Yost. "The Ethnobotany of the Waorani of Eastern Ecuador." *Botanical Museum Leaflets/Harvard University*. Summer 1983.

_____."The Ethnomedicine of the Waorani of Amazonian Ecuador." *Journal of Ethnopharmacology*, Vol. 9, 1983.

Dufour, Darna L. "Use of Tropical Rainforests by Native Amazonians."

BioScience. October 1990.

Kaplan, Jon and James Larrick. "Workup on the Waorani." *Natural History*. Vol. 93, No. 9, 1984.

Mardon, Mark. "Piercing the Jungle's Heart." *Sierra*. March/April 1990.

Yost, James A. "Community Development and Ethnic Survival: The Wao Case." (A paper presented to Society for Applied Anthropology in the symposium "Community Developments for Minority Language Groups.") April 1978.

_____."Variables Affecting Land Requirements for Tropical Forest Horticulturalists: Some Policy Implications." Summer Institute of Linguistics. 1987.

FILMS

"Nomads of the Rainforest," *Nova*, November 6, 1984 (PBS).

Tell Them We Are Not Auca: We Are Waorani, International Media Services, Summer Institute of Linguistics, Dallas, 1988.

INDEX

tree climbing, 29

United States, 60

ABOUT THE AUTHOR

Alexandra Siy's interest in the natural world began during the first celebration of Earth Day, when she was ten years old. She studied biology in college and went on to do research in a biotechnology laboratory. Later she earned a master's degree in science education and taught high school biology and physiology.

Ms. Siy, who lives in Albany, New York, now divides her time between writing and raising her two young children. **Global Villages** continues the theme of the interconnectedness of people and the environment, which she began in the **Circle of Life**, her first group of books for Dillon Press.